First Person
A ★ M ★ E ★ R ★ I ★ C ★ A

THE ALLIES AGAINST THE AXIS

World War II (1940-1950)

Richard Steins

Twenty-First Century Books

A Division of Henry Holt and Company
New York

Twenty-First Century Books
A Division of Henry Holt and Company, Inc.
115 West 18th Street
New York, New York 10011

Henry Holt® and colophon are trademarks of Henry Holt and
Company, Inc.
Publishers since 1866

©1993 by Blackbirch Graphics, Inc.
First Edition
5 4 3 2 1

Published in Canada by Fitzhenry & Whiteside Ltd.
195 Allstate Parkway, Markham, Ontario L3R 4T8

Printed in the United States of America
All first editions are printed on acid-free paper ∞.

Created and produced in association with Blackbirch Graphics, Inc.

Library of Congress Cataloging-in-Publication Data

Steins, Richard.
    The Allies against the Axis: World War II (1940–1950) / Richard Steins.
        p.   cm. — (First person America)
    Includes bibliographical references and index.
    ISBN 0-8050-2586-3
    1. World War, 1939–1945—Sources—Juvenile literature.   [1. World
    War, 1939–1945—Sources.] I. Title. II. Series.
    D743.7.S75   1993
    940.53—dc20

                                                            93-24997
                                                               CIP
                                                                AC

CONTENTS

INTRODUCTION

At his renomination in 1936, President Franklin D. Roosevelt said "This generation of Americans has a rendezvous with destiny." His words were prophetic. Only four years after he spoke them, the United States entered what was to be one of the most tumultuous decades in its history.

In 1940, most people in the country desired nothing more than to stay out of the war that was already raging in Europe between Germany and Great Britain and France. The 1930s had been a time of severe testing for the United States, as the effects of the Great Depression left millions of people unemployed and without hope. Roosevelt had given the nation hope once again, but he knew that eventually, the United States would have to enter the war. In this volume you will hear the voice of an American businessman who believed passionately that the United States should never get involved in European affairs. And you will see the opposing view of President Roosevelt, who knew that he had to persuade the American people that they actually had a vital interest in what happened overseas.

War came suddenly and unexpectedly, not in Europe but in the Pacific. On Sunday, December 7, 1941, Japanese fighters, dive bombers, and torpedo planes bombed the American navy stationed at Pearl Harbor,

Hawaii. Congress declared war on Japan the next day, and on December 11, Germany declared war on the United States.

The "Axis"—the alliance between Germany, Japan, and Italy—was now set to battle the "Allies"—principally the United States, Great Britain, and France, although dozens of other free nations of the world eventually joined the fight. The United States struck back at Japan, in a daring air raid over Tokyo on April 18, 1942. The words of a pilot who took part in that dangerous mission appear in Chapter Two. You will also read the personal remembrances of two of America's top military leaders, General Dwight D. Eisenhower and General Douglas MacArthur, and get

President Franklin D. Roosevelt signs the declaration of war against Japan, December 1941 (*Library of Congress*).

5

a glimpse of the correspondence between Roosevelt and British Prime Minister Winston Churchill.

America's involvement in World War II lasted from 1941 until 1945. During that time, people's lives all over the country were changed forever. More than 16 million men entered the army, navy, and marines to wage war in Europe and the Pacific. At home, millions of women joined the workforce for the first time, contributing to the Allied cause by taking up many jobs in factories and offices that had previously been done by the men now in the service. Whether serving as welders, riveters, machinists, or truck drivers, women played a vital role in the victory that came in 1945.

Some Americans were victims of grave injustices committed by the U.S. government during the war years. Nearly 120,000 people of Japanese ancestry—a majority of them American citizens—who were living on the West Coast were rounded up and shipped to concentration camps, simply because of their Japanese heritage. A survivor recalls the horror of that very painful experience in a selection printed in Chapter Three.

Because of the need to divert as many materials into the military services as possible, people in civilian life faced shortages. Items such as gasoline and meat were rationed—a person could buy only a limited amount of these goods each month. Other items, such as

A World War II propaganda poster warns Americans of the Axis threat (*National Archives*).

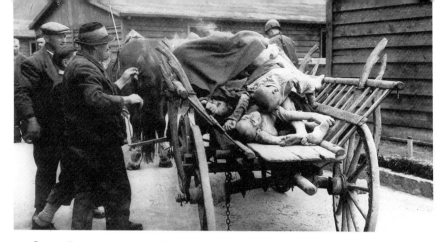

Bodies of Holocaust victims lie piled in a cart at a concentration camp in Austria, 1945 (*National Archives*).

nylon that was used to make women's stockings, were completely unavailable. But life went on. Americans listened to popular music, went to the movies, and watched as their favorite stars went abroad to entertain the troops. The whole country yearned for the day when peace would finally come.

At war's end, some 290,000 American troops had died in combat. The number was small compared to the 20 million Soviet citizens who perished during the brutal Nazi invasion and occupation of Russia and the more than 6 million Jews who had perished in Nazi concentration camps. The America of 1945 was a country that had "grown up" as a result of depression and war.

The war ended as suddenly as it had begun—with the mushroom-shaped clouds of atomic bombs dropped by the United States on the Japanese cities of Hiroshima and Nagasaki.

When Japan surrendered, Roosevelt had already been dead for four months. Exhausted and ill after twelve years in the presidency, he died of a stroke on April 12, 1945, and was succeeded by Harry S Truman. In a passage excerpted in Chapter Five, Truman describes what happened the day he found out he had become president.

Joyful Americans celebrate Japan's unconditional surrender on August 14, 1945 (*National Archives*).

Truman led the nation during the last half of the 1940s—another period of enormous change. America now faced a challenge posed by its former ally, the Soviet Union. Truman and most of his advisors believed that the Soviets posed a major threat to Europe and the United States. Winston Churchill echoed these feelings in a speech in 1946 at Westminster College in Missouri, where he coined the famous phrase "iron curtain" to describe the deep division between the democratic countries of Western Europe and the United States and the opposing Soviet Union and its allies.

The Truman administration developed the policy of "containment"—which meant not going to war but still trying to contain the expansion of Soviet power. It also instituted the "Truman Doctrine," giving foreign aid to nations that were trying to resist communism within their own borders. The thoughts of Truman are reprinted in Chapter Four.

Finally, as the decade neared its end, America saw Harry Truman fighting valiantly to be re-elected to the presidency in 1948. In the final chapter are passages on Truman's campaign and the experiences of a former soldier who has finally come home after years at war.

CHAPTER 1

THE THREAT
OF WAR

America's Policy
of Isolation

In his farewell address to the nation in 1796, President George Washington (1732-1799) warned the United States not to get involved in the affairs of foreign nations—especially the nations of Europe. Although this advice was well-intentioned, Washington did not foresee the complications of world politics more than a hundred years later.

In 1917, the United States declared war on Germany and sent American soldiers to fight in France. That great conflict—World War I—ended in 1918. Despite U.S. participation in this war, the overwhelming majority of Americans continued to believe that the United States should steer clear of Europe's many problems. People who believed in not getting involved in another country's affairs were known as "isolationists." They favored the "isolation" of the United States from

Adolf Hitler leads a Nazi rally in Nuremberg, Germany, 1928 (*National Gallery*).

European conflicts. Those who believed that America had to get involved overseas, for whatever reason, were considered "interventionists."

In 1933, Adolf Hitler's Nazi Party came to power in Germany. The German dictator persecuted not only Jews within Germany, he also threatened to seize territories of neighboring countries that he believed belonged to Germany. When Hitler (1889-1945) invaded Poland in September 1939, Europe was plunged into World War II.

President Franklin D. Roosevelt (1882-1945) understood that the United States could not remain neutral forever. The huge Atlantic Ocean would no longer be an effective protective barrier from Hitler's bombers.

Nevertheless, even as late as 1940—when France had fallen to the German invaders and Britain was being pounded by Nazi bombs—most Americans believed passionately that the United States must continue to remain neutral.

In the selection printed here, Robert Wood, a prominent American businessman and World War I veteran, argues in 1940 that the Atlantic Ocean *is* a sufficient protection against the German army, and that America's true interests are in North and South America, not in Europe.

Robert Wood on Leaving Europe Alone

There are two schools of thought in this country on the subject of our foreign policy. They may be termed "Interventionists" and "Isolationists." . . .

So on every count it seems inconceivable to me that Germany at the end of the war, even if aided by its allies, who will be in a worse condition of exhaustion than Germany itself, will attack the United States. And if this country with its 130,000,000 people and its two great natural ocean barriers cannot defend itself unaided by Britain or anybody else, it does not deserve to survive. The great nation that has to trust to others for its defense is on the downward path to destruction. . . .

Americans like myself feel that our true mission is in North America and South America. We stand today in an unrivalled position. With our resources and organizing ability we can develop with our Canadian friends, an only partially developed continent like North America and a virgin continent like South America. The reorganization and proper development of Mexico alone would afford an outlet for our capital and energies for some time to come.

From: Robert E. Wood, "Our Foreign Policy: The Course We Are Pursuing Leads to War," in *Vital Speeches of the Day*, vol. VII. (Washington D.C.: Government Printing Office, 1944).

American opinion about intervention changed, literally, in one day—after the Japanese attack on Pearl Harbor, Hawaii, on December 7, 1941. From that moment forward, America was once again at war.

Franklin Delano
Roosevelt, portrait by
American painter Henry
Salem Hubbell (*National
Portrait Gallery*).

A Rallying Cry

By 1941, President Franklin D. Roosevelt (FDR) knew that the United States was in danger—not only from the threat of Hitler's aggression in Europe, but also from the militaristic government of Japan, which was invading and intimidating other countries in the Western Pacific.

But FDR could not lead the American people where they refused to go. Most of the country remained strongly isolationist, despite the wars that raged on both sides of the world.

What Roosevelt could do, however, was to teach his people about the principles of freedom, in the hope that public opinion would eventually come to see what America's stake in the world was. On January 6, 1941,

Roosevelt went before the U.S. Congress and delivered his "Four Freedoms" speech. In it, he warned that U.S. security was in deep danger, and that a safe world could only be assured if certain freedoms were guaranteed: the freedom of speech, the freedom of religion, the freedom from want, and the freedom from fear.

Franklin D. Roosevelt Speaks About "The Four Freedoms"

I address you, the Members of this new Congress, at a moment unprecedented in the history of the union. I use the word "unprecedented" because at no previous time has American security been as seriously threatened from without as it is today. . . .

I suppose that every realist knows that the democratic way of life is at this moment being directly assailed in every part of the world—assailed either by arms or by secret spreading of poisonous propaganda by those who seek to destroy unity and promote discord in nations still at peace.

During sixteen long months this assault has blotted out the whole pattern of democratic life in an appalling number of independent nations, great and small.

In the future days which we seek to make secure, we look forward to a world founded upon four essential human freedoms.

The first is freedom of speech and expression—everywhere in the world.

The second is freedom of every person to worship God in his own way—everywhere in the world.

The third is freedom from want, which, translated into world terms, means economic understandings which will secure to every nation a healthy peacetime life for its inhabitants—everywhere in the world.

The fourth is freedom from fear. Which, translated into world terms, means a worldwide reduction of armaments to such a point and in such a thorough fashion that no nation will be in a position to commit an act of physical aggression against any neighbor—anywhere in the world.

From: Transcription in *The New York Times* January 7, 1941.

In the end, it was not Roosevelt's eloquent words that turned American opinion around, but Japanese bombs and torpedoes, which slammed into American warships at Pearl Harbor, Hawaii, on Sunday, December 7, 1941. This surprise attack shocked the nation. The following day, Roosevelt went before the Congress and asked for a declaration of war against Japan. The famous statement that follows describes the day of the attack as a "date which will live in infamy." The attack also represented America's rude awakening from the unrealistic belief that it could always remain isolated from the world.

Franklin D. Roosevelt's Address to Congress (1941)

Yesterday, December 7, 1941—a date which will live in infamy—the United States of America was suddenly and deliberately attacked by naval and air forces of the empire of Japan.

The United States was at peace with that nation, and, at the solicitation of Japan, was still in conversation with its government and its Emperor looking toward the maintenance of peace in the Pacific. Indeed, one hour after Japanese air squadrons had commenced bombing in the American island of Oahu, the Japanese Ambassador to the United States and his colleague delivered to the Secretary of State a formal reply to a recent American message. And, while this reply stated that it seemed useless to continue the existing diplomatic negotiations, it contained no threat or hint of war or armed attack.

It will be recorded that the distance of Hawaii from Japan makes it obvious that the attack was deliberately planned many days or even weeks ago. During the intervening time the Japanese Government has deliberately sought to deceive the United States by false statements and expressions of hope for continued peace.

The attack yesterday on the Hawaiian Islands has caused severe damage to American naval and military forces. I regret to tell you that very many American lives have been lost. In addition American ships have been reported torpedoed on the high seas between San Francisco and Honolulu.

From: Transcription in *The New York Times* December 9, 1941.

President Roosevelt ended his speech by announcing that he had directed the army and the navy to take all measures necessary to defend the United States.

Smoke and flames pour out of the *U.S.S. West Virginia* (foreground) and the *U.S.S. Tennessee* during the Japanese attack on Pearl Harbor, December 7, 1941 (*UPI/Bettmann Photos*).

Sudden Attack in Hawaii

In the 1920s, Japan was a poor, agricultural country with no natural resources. Most of its people were barely able to make a living. But despite its poverty, Japan had a huge army whose leaders were eager for foreign conquest.

Gradually, during the early 1930s, the Japanese military assumed more and more control over the civilian government and began to enact their plan to make Japan the leading power in the Western Pacific.

In 1940, a year after war broke out in Europe, Japan signed a treaty of alliance with Nazi Germany. In the same year, it declared the existence of the "Greater East Asia Co-Prosperity Sphere," which in reality meant that Japan intended to dominate all countries in East Asia. One of the first measures the Japanese military took in 1940 was to invade Indochina, a colony of the French. France had just been invaded and defeated by Nazi Germany.

Japan's ambitions in Asia were alarming to the government of the United States, which looked on almost powerlessly as the Japanese rampaged through Asia. The American colony of the Philippines was perilously close to Japanese-occupied Indochina.

Short of going to war, the U.S. government imposed an embargo on oil to Japan in 1941. Such a measure was a serious blow to the Japanese military. Having no oil at all, Japan depended totally on foreign imports. Without oil, Japanese trucks and tanks would grind to a halt.

In late 1941, the military assumed full control of the Japanese government and made a secret decision to attack the U.S. fleet anchored at Pearl Harbor, Hawaii. With the American navy knocked out of action, the military leaders reasoned, Japan could invade most of the nations of East Asia without interference.

The Japanese apparently believed that the Americans would not have the will to fight a long war and would eventually make peace. It was a disastrous miscalculation on their part, one that led to the total defeat of Japan and to the deaths of millions of people.

Sunday, December 7, 1941, was a warm, lazy day in the Hawaiian islands. The following piece describes "Battleship Row" at Pearl Harbor when Japanese fighters appeared and the bombs began falling.

The Chaos of Pearl Harbor

Ensign Joe Taussig, officer of the deck, pulled the alarm bell. The ship's bugler got ready to blow general quarters, but Taussig took the bugle and tossed it overboard. Somehow it seemed too much like make-believe at a time like this. Instead he shouted over the PA system again and again, "All hands, general quarters, Air raid! This is no drill!". . .

The *Oklahoma's* call to arms needed no extra punch. First came an air raid alert; then general quarters a minute later. This time the voice on the PA system added a few well-chosen words, which one crew member recalls as follows: "Real planes, real bombs; this is no drill!" Other witnesses have a less delicate version of the last part. The language alone, they say, convinced them that this was it.

A few skeptics still held out. In the *Honolulu's* hoist room Private Roy Henry bet another Marine a dollar that it was the Army, pulling a surprise on the Navy with dummy torpedoes. The men in the repair ship *Rigel's* pipe and copper shop remained unperturbed when a seaman wearing only underwear burst in with the news—they figured the fellow was pretending he was crazy so he could get back to the Coast. . . .

Down the corridors . . . up the ladders . . . through the hatches the men ran, climbed, milled, and shoved toward their battle stations. And it was high time. The alarm was no sooner given when the *Oklahoma* took the first of five torpedoes . . . the *West Virginia* the first of six. . . . Next the *Arizona* took two, even though a little to the north and partly blocked by the *Vestal*. Then the *California* got two, even though far to the south and a relatively poor target. Only the inboard battleships seemed safe— *Maryland* alongside *Oklahoma* and *Tennessee* beside *West Virginia*.

From: *Day of Infamy* by Walter Lord (New York: Henry Holt & Co., 1957). Reprinted by permission.

CHAPTER 2

ECHOES OF BATTLE

The American Response

Immediately after their surprise attack on the American fleet in Hawaii on December 7, 1941, the Japanese military launched a series of all-out offensives throughout East Asia and the Western Pacific. Within a matter of months, Japan had conquered the American colony of the Philippines, all the Dutch East Indies, and the Malayan Peninsula, including the British crown colony of Singapore.

It was a dark time for the United States and its allies, and the American people desperately needed a dramatic victory to turn things around and lift their morale.

On April 18, 1942—four months after the war began—Colonel James Doolittle (1896–1993) boarded his B-25 bomber aboard the U.S. aircraft carrier *Hornet* in the Western Pacific and took off for Tokyo. Accompanying him was a squadron of other B-25s on a daring mission: the first American bombing raid on Tokyo.

Three of the B-25s were shot down over Japan and their pilots were captured. The rest went on to land in China. Despite the losses, Doolittle's raid was a stunning success. The Japanese people had been told by their government that not one bomb would ever fall on Tokyo. When Doolittle's planes appeared in the skies over Tokyo, everyone—the Japanese people as well as the government—was deeply shaken.

The selection that follows presents the recollections of Ted Lawson, a pilot who flew with Doolittle's raiders.

Colonel James Doolittle led the first American raid on Japan after Pearl Harbor (*Wide World Photos*).

Ted Lawson Remembers the Bombing of Tokyo

I was almost on the first of our objectives before I saw it. I gave the engines full throttle as Davenport adjusted the prop pitch to get a better grip on the air. We climbed as quickly as possible to 1,500 feet, in the manner which we had practiced for a month and had discussed for three additional weeks.

There was just time to get up there, level off, attend to the routine of opening the bomb bay, make a short run and let fly with the first bomb. The red light blinked on my instrument board, and I knew the first 500-pounder had gone.

Our speed was picking up. The red light blinked again, and I knew Clever had let the second bomb go. Just as the light blinked, a black cloud appeared. . .in front of us and rushed past at great speed. Two more appeared ahead of us, on about the line of our wingtips, and they too swept past. They had our altitude perfectly, but they were leading us too much.

The third red light flickered, and, since we were now over a flimsy area in the southern part of the city, the fourth light blinked. That was the incendiary, which I knew would separate as soon as it hit the wind and that dozens of small fire bombs would molt from it.

From: Bombing of Tokyo, 1942, *Thirty Seconds Over Tokyo*, by Ted Lawson (New York: Penguin Books, 1944). Reprinted by permission.

An Exchange Between Friends

World War II produced two great Allied leaders: Franklin D. Roosevelt, president of the United States, and Winston Churchill (1874-1965), prime minister of Great Britain.

Roosevelt and Churchill were both "navy men." Churchill had been First Sea Lord of the Admiralty during World War I. Roosevelt's first job in the federal government was assistant secretary of the Navy during World War I.

In September 1939, immediately after the outbreak of World War II, after many years out of power, Churchill was recalled at the age of 64 to again head the admiralty. Roosevelt wrote a letter to Churchill congratulating him on his return to government. It was highly unusual for a head of one state to correspond directly with a cabinet-level minister in another government. But Roosevelt was interested in naval matters and knew the important role that naval power would play in the coming war.

In May 1940, Churchill became prime minister. Roosevelt and Churchill finally met in August 1941 on a ship off the coast of Nova Scotia, Canada. By now Britain had been at war with Germany for almost two years. The United States was still officially neutral, although Roosevelt had been supplying old ships and other material to the British.

After the United States entered World War II in December 1941, Churchill and Roosevelt's correspondence became more frequent. By the spring of 1942, just a few months after America joined the fighting, Churchill wrote to Roosevelt to report on the progress of the war. In his letter of April 1, 1942, he explains that the Allies are doing everything they can to get supplies to the Russians through the Arctic port of Murmansk. Churchill also points out that the new bombing techniques used on the German cities of Essen, Cologne, and Lübeck have inflicted damage on the same massive scale of the German fire-bombing of the British city of Coventry in the fall of 1940.

In his brief response to Churchill on April 3, 1942, Roosevelt states that the Allies *must* eventually open a front in the west to relieve the pressure on the Russians. (On November 8, 1942, American and British troops landed in Morocco and Algeria, in North Africa. This invasion, known as Operation Torch, was the first Allied ground attack on German forces from the West. It was led by American General Dwight D. Eisenhower.)

Winston Churchill (left) and Franklin Roosevelt meet at the White House in December 1941 (*Wide World Photos*).

Churchill to Roosevelt, April 1, 1942

Delighted by your letter of March 18 just received. I am so grateful for all your thoughts about my affairs, and personal kindness....

I am looking forward to receiving your plan. We are working very hard here, not only at plans but at preparations....

All now depends upon the vast Russo-German struggle. It looks as if the heavy German offensive may not break until after the middle of May or the beginning of June. We are doing all we can to help and also to take the weight off. We shall have to fight every convoy through to Murmansk. Stalin is pleased with our deliveries. They are due to go up fifty percent after June and it will be very difficult to do this in view of the new war and also of shipping. Only the weather is holding us back from continuous heavy bombing attack on Germany. Our new methods are most successful. Essen, Cologne, and above all Lübeck were all on the Coventry scale. I am sure it is most important to keep this up all through the summer, blasting Hitler from behind while he is grappling with the Bear. Everything that you can send to weight our attack will be of the utmost value. At Malta also we are containing, with much hard fighting, nearly six hundred German and Italian planes. I am wondering whether these will move to the south Russian front in the near future. There are many rumours of an airborne attack on Malta, possibly this month.

Having heard from Stalin that he is expecting the Germans would use gas on him, I have assured him that we shall treat any such outrage as if directed upon us, and will retaliate without limit. This we are in a good position to do. I propose at his desire to announce this toward the end of the present month and we are using the interval to work up our own precautions. Please let all the above be absolutely between ourselves....

My wife and I both send our kindest regards to you and Mrs. Roosevelt. Perhaps when the weather gets better I may propose myself for a weekend with you and flip over. We have so much to settle that would go easily in talk.

○ ○ ○

Roosevelt to Churchill, April 3, 1942

Dear Winston,

What Harry and Geo. Marshall will tell you all about has my heart and *mind* in it. Your people and mine demand the establishment of a front to draw off pressure on the Russians, and these peoples are wise enough to see that the Russians are today killing more Germans and destroying more equipment than you and I put together. Even if full success is not attained, the *big* objective will be.

Go to it! Syria and Egypt will be made more secure, even if the Germans find out about our plans.

Best of luck. Make Harry go to bed early, and let him obey Dr. Fulton, USN, whom I am sending with him as supernurse with full authority.

From: *Roosevelt and Churchill: Their Secret Wartime Correspondence*, Francis L. Loewenheim, Harold D. Langley, and Manfred Jonas, eds. (New York: DaCapo Press, 1975). Reprinted by permission.

The War in Europe

Dwight David Eisenhower (1890-1969) was born in Denison, Texas. When he was less than one year old, his family moved to Abilene, Kansas. Eisenhower, known to friends since childhood by his nickname "Ike," graduated from West Point in 1915. He then served in a variety of army posts, including a tour in the Philippines from 1935-1940.

Eisenhower distinguished himself as a leader capable of resolving conflict among his subordinates. He was promoted quickly after America's entry into World War II in 1941, rising from the rank of colonel to general in two years.

Eisenhower's first challenge as a field commander came when he was assigned to lead Operation Torch, the Allied invasion of North Africa. This campaign had three goals: to strike back at German ground forces for the first time in the war, to drive the German army out of North Africa, and to relieve the pressure on the Soviet Union, which had been the only Allied power fighting the Germans on the ground.

Operation Torch began on November 8, 1942, with Allied landings in Morocco and Algeria. By May of 1943, all German forces in North Africa had surrendered. Because of this success, Eisenhower became the supreme commander of the Western Allied Forces in December 1943—the multinational army that was preparing to invade German-occupied France the following year.

Dwight David Eisenhower, portrait by American painter Thomas Edgar Stephens (*National Portrait Gallery*).

American troops land on the beaches of Normandy, France, during the D-Day invasion on June 6, 1944 (*National Archives*).

Eisenhower's strategy to defeat Germany began with the invasion of France on June 6, 1944 (D-Day). By August, Paris had been liberated and the Allied armies were poised to move into Germany. In the selection that follows, Eisenhower describes the D-Day invasion and remembers a victory that changed the course of World War II.

Eisenhower Recalls the War

The first report came from the airborne units I had visited only a few hours earlier and was most encouraging in tone. As the morning wore on it became apparent that the landing was going fairly well. Montgomery took off in a destroyer to visit the beaches and to find a place in which to set up his own advanced headquarters. I promised to visit him on the following day.

Operations in the Utah area, which involved the co-ordination of the amphibious landing with the American airborne operation, proceeded satisfactorily, as did those on the extreme left flank. The day's reports, however, showed that extremely fierce fighting had developed in the Omaha sector. That was the spot, I decided, to which I would proceed the next morning.

We made the trip in a destroyer and upon arrival found that the 1st and 29th Divisions, assaulting on Omaha, had finally dislodged the enemy and were proceeding swiftly inland. Isolated centers of resistance still held out and some of them sustained a most annoying artillery fire against our beaches and landing ships. I had a chance to confer with General Bradley and found him, as always, stout-hearted and confident of the result. In point of fact the resistance encountered on Omaha Beach was at about the level we had feared all along the line. The conviction of the German that we would not attack in the weather then prevailing was a definite factor in the degree of surprise we achieved and accounted to some extent for the low order of active opposition on most of the beaches. In the Omaha sector an alert enemy division, the 352d, which prisoners stated had been in the area on maneuvers and defense exercises, accounted for some of the intense fighting in that locality....

The next few days thoroughly taxed the soundness of the build-up plan that had been so patiently devised over many months. On the whole it stood the strain exceedingly well, but here and there emergency conditions of the battlefield demanded minor changes in plan and my location at Portsmouth enabled these to be executed swiftly and smoothly.

From: *Dwight D. Eisenhower, Crusade in Europe* (New York: Doubleday, 1948). Reprinted by permission.

The Challenges of Army Segregation

During World War II, the armed forces of the United States continued to be racially segregated. Whites and African Americans served in separate units in all branches of the service, with the exception of the Marine Corps. African Americans had served in the military as far back as the Revolutionary War. During the Civil War, President Abraham Lincoln encouraged the formation of all-black units to help in the struggle against the Confederacy.

In 1942, the Women's Army Auxiliary Corps (WAAC) was formed—the first time women were allowed to officially wear uniforms and hold rank. As with the men's units, the first WAAC units were required to be racially segregated. (The WAAC existed for one year and then, in 1943, was changed to WAC as part of the U.S. Army.)

The first African-American woman to be commissioned as an officer in the WAAC was Charity Adams Earley, a young Southerner who had been a school teacher before enlisting. After being commissioned, she and the other black women in her graduating class were sent to an army post near Des Moines, Iowa.

The army was not sure what to do with women enlistees—black or white. As a result, Earley faced

This poster, printed by the United States Army, was designed to motivate women to join the Women's Army Auxiliary Corps during World War II (*National Archives*).

double discrimination, first as an African American and then as a woman. Eventually she was assigned to help run a training unit for black female enlistees. Within a matter of months, more than 1,000 African-American women had joined the WAAC, and Earley played an important role in training them for their future duties. As the war progressed, WAAC troops were used in noncombat positions—as secretaries, cooks, drivers, bakers, and teachers, to name just a few of their jobs.

Although relatively few black women served in uniform during World War II, hundreds of thousands of black men enlisted or were drafted. Some units served in combat with bravery and distinction in Europe and the Pacific. In 1947, President Harry S Truman (1884–1972) ended all racial segregation in the U.S. armed forces by presidential decree.

In the selection that follows, Earley describes what life was like for an African-American woman in uniform. She relates the story of her first visit to her family late in 1942 and the experiences she had as a black female officer on the train ride home.

Charity Adams Earley

There were...several unpleasant events associated with my first visit back to my hometown. The Carolina Special, of the Southern Railway system, was segregated, as were all trains and other accommodations in the South.... I had boarded the train at night in Cincinnati, and the following morning I went to the dining car and joined the line of people waiting for a seat. When the line moved, I moved, and I finally made it to the door of the dining car when the steward put his arm across the door and announced that the car was full. I stood there in front of the line and waited. After a rather long time the steward called, "All persons in uniform first." I stepped forward. He thrust his arm across the door again and said, angrily, "I said all persons in uniform first." Before I could answer, I heard a voice behind me.

"Well, what in the hell do you think that is that she has on? Get your _____ arm down before I break it off for you."

The voice was so obviously southern that I turned around in surprise. That voice belonged to a very tall, very blond second lieutenant, and he was so angry that his face was quite red. He continued to talk, and loudly. "What in the world are we fighting this damned war for? She's giving her service, too, and can eat anywhere I can. And, by Jesus, I am going to eat with her in this diner."

By this time I was rather alarmed and wondered what would happen next. When I looked at the steward, he had stepped aside and was waiting to show me to my seat. I followed him to the middle of the diner where he seated me at a table for four. The lieutenant came right behind and sat down opposite me.... We did have breakfast together, and as we ate, the officer kept up his tirade against "crackers" and "cheap whites" and "what this war is all about." He did all the talking, and when the meal was over, he escorted me back to my seat, bowed and left. I never saw him again, but I still think of him as a southern gentleman.

From: Charity Adams Earley, *One Woman's Army: A Black Officer Remembers the WAAC* (Galveston: Texas A&M University Press, 1989). Reprinted by permission.

Surrender

The war between the United States and Japan threatened to be long and bloody. After spectacular successes early in 1942, the Japanese armed forces suddenly found themselves on the defensive. The United States quickly regained the initiative and slowly, island by island, began to push the Japanese back toward their mainland.

But the Japanese troops were courageous and loyal to their emperor. As part of Japanese tradition, they almost never surrendered, which meant that U.S. forces had to fight for each Pacific island inch by inch.

By the middle of 1945 the American army and navy stood at the gates of the Japanese mainland. (Germany had already surrendered on May 7, 1945.) The planned invasion of Japan promised to be the most horrible and brutal action of the entire war. But suddenly, in a matter of days, the war was over. The United States dropped its secret weapon on Japan—the atomic bomb. Two cities, Hiroshima and Nagasaki, were destroyed in early August 1945.

Finally realizing that their situation was hopeless, the Japanese surrendered unconditionally on August 14, 1945. The formal surrender ceremony took place on the deck of the battleship *U.S.S. Missouri* in Tokyo Bay on September 2, 1945.

Speaking for the Allies was U.S. General Douglas MacArthur (1880-1964), who only four years earlier had been forced to leave his command in the Philippines before the advancing Japanese army. In the

Above: Nagasaki before the atomic bomb was dropped. *Below:* The exact same area, after the explosion (*National Archives*).

selection that follows, MacArthur sets the tone for the occasion with a dignified speech that invites the Japanese delegates to sign the document of surrender.

The surrender ceremony was both a real and a symbolic event, one that clearly demonstrated the Allied victory, the end to Japanese aggression in the Pacific, and the return to peace throughout the world.

General MacArthur on Victory

"We are gathered here, representatives of the major warring powers, to conclude a solemn agreement whereby peace may be restored. The issues, involving divergent ideals and ideologies have been determined on the battlefields of the world and hence are not for our discussion or debate. Nor is it for us here to meet, representing as we do a majority of the people of the earth, in a spirit of distrust, malice or hatred. But rather it is for us, both victors and vanquished, to rise to that higher dignity which alone befits the sacred purposes we are about to serve, committing all our people unreservedly to faithful compliance with the obligation they are here formally to assume.

"It is my earnest hope and indeed the hope of all mankind that from this solemn occasion a better world shall emerge out of the blood and carnage of the past—a world founded upon faith and understanding—a world dedicated to the dignity of man and the fulfillment of his most cherished wish—for freedom, tolerance and justice.

"The terms and conditions upon which the surrender of the Japanese Imperial Forces is here to be given and accepted are contained in the instrument of surrender now before you.

"As Supreme Commander for the Allied Powers, I announce it my firm purpose, in the tradition of the countries I represent, to proceed in the discharge of my responsibilities with justice and tolerance, while taking all necessary dispositions to insure that the terms of surrender are fully promptly and faithfully complied with."

From: *Reminiscences* by Douglas MacArthur (New York: McGraw-Hill, 1964). Reprinted by permission.

CHAPTER 3

THE WAR AT HOME

Fear and Paranoia

At the outbreak of the war with Japan in 1941, nearly 120,000 people of Japanese ancestry lived on the West Coast, most of them in California. About two-thirds of them were native-born American citizens who were descendants of Japanese immigrants who had migrated to the United States beginning in the 1890s. They were mostly farmers and shopkeepers.

The Japanese Americans—known as "Nisei"—were the object of resentment and racial hatred long before World War II began. But when the war broke out, certain politicians whipped up the rage and fears of white Californians by calling for a forced evacuation of all Japanese from the West Coast. Numerous patriotic organizations and newspapers pressured the govern-

A Japanese-American family awaits final evacuation from their home in California in 1942. Photograph by Dorothea Lange (*National Archives*).

ment to such a degree that in February 1942, President Roosevelt signed an order for the evacuation of all Japanese on the West Coast.

Despite the fact that there was no evidence of disloyalty among the Nisei, they were forced to leave their homes and jobs on one month's notice to be relocated in concentration camps in the West and Midwest. They were instructed to sell all of their property at whatever price they could get and were herded onto uncomfortable trains for the long trip to the interior.

Once in the camps, the Japanese Americans endured severe hardships. They lived in drafty barracks and ate in mess halls and were forced to shower in groups. The Japanese Americans had always considered themselves loyal Americans and were depressed, bewildered, and angry at the way their government was treating them.

The Nisei were gradually released from their imprisonment as the shock of Pearl Harbor wore off. But by then it was 1944, and many returned to their hometowns without property and with few prospects for the future.

The internment of Japanese Americans was a terrible violation of free people's rights during World War II. In 1988, in recognition of the mistake made by the U.S. government, Congress authorized the payment of $20,000 to each survivor of the forced evacuation. It was a small step on the part of the government to correct an injustice committed during the frightening years of World War II.

In the selection printed here, a Japanese American who survived the imprisonment describes what it was like to be forced to leave one's home on short notice and to be relocated to a concentration camp.

Recollections of a Nisei

"Right after Pearl Harbor we had no idea what was going to happen, but toward the end of December we started hearing rumors and talk of the evacuation (having) started. We could tell from what we read in the newspapers and the propaganda they were printing.... So we were expecting something and the evacuation was no great surprise.

"Once the evacuation was decided, we were told we had about a month to get rid of our property or do whatever we wanted to with it.

"We could take only what we could carry, and most of us were carrying two suitcases or duffel bags....

"I had a savings account that was left intact, but people who had their money in the Japanese bank in Seattle had their assets frozen from Pearl Harbor until the late 1960s, when the funds were finally released. They received no interest. . . .

"They had also built barbed-wire fences around the camp, with a tower on each corner with military personnel and machine guns, rifles, and searchlights. It was terrifying because we didn't know what was going to happen to us. We didn't know where we were going and we were just doing what we were told. No questions asked. If you get an order, you go ahead and do it.

"When we got to Twin Falls, we were loaded onto trucks again, and we looked around and all we could see was that vast desert with nothing but sagebrush.... The barracks had been built and the kitchen facilities were there, but the laundry room, showers, and latrines were not finished.... When the wind blew, it was dusty and we had to wear face masks to go to the dining hall. When winter came and it rained, the dust turned into gumbo mud. Until the latrines were finished, we had to use outhouses.

From: *The Home Front: An Oral History of the War Years in America: 1941–45* by Archie Satterfield (New York: Playboy Press, 1981). Reprinted by permission.

I'm Proud... my husband wants me to do my part

SEE YOUR U. S. EMPLOYMENT SERVICE
WAR MANPOWER COMMISSION

A government poster printed during the war encourages women to work in factories to help the war effort (*National Archives*).

Women Work for Victory

During World War II, more than 16 million men enlisted in or were drafted into the armed forces of the United States. Most of them had to serve in uniform until the war ended, almost four years after it began.

Such a huge shift of population into the military meant that many civilian jobs held by men needed to be filled. During the war, thousands of these jobs, whether in factories or offices, were taken by women, most of whom had never held paying jobs before. Among the many changes brought on by the war was the increased number of women in the workplace. In 1941, women made up 24 percent of the total workforce. In 1945, that number had risen to 36 percent.

"Rosie the Riveter" was a Norman Rockwell painting of a woman working in a factory riveting bolts to the wing of an airplane. It appeared on the cover of the *Saturday Evening Post* in the early years of the war. "Rosie" became the symbol of women pitching in to help win the war by doing what had been "men's" jobs. A majority of the women discovered that they liked working. Receiving a regular paycheck helped make up the loss of salary they suffered when fathers, husbands, and brothers went off to war. These women also found that working toward a common goal did much to lift morale on the home front.

Mable Gerken, a typical "Rosie the Riveter," kept a diary of her experiences as a factory worker during World War II. In the excerpt that follows, she describes the pride she felt in her work, as well as her realization that America would need to adjust to new racial attitudes after the war. Side by side with white women in the factory were more and more African Americans, who would also want to claim their rightful place among those who had helped to win the war.

A woman works on the construction of a ship at Kaiser Shipyards in Richmond, California, 1943 (*National Archives*).

The Female Factory Experience, 1943

February 24, 1943. Things are very confusing here, whether accidentally or on purpose. The first day, I opened the log book where we enter our parts, and at the top of the page I read: "Receiving point 6B is in the southeast end of the building. You will be asked a hundred times a day." And I guess I have at that. This is receiving point 6A. Across the aisle is receiving point 4A. They are in the center of the building. We call them receiving points, not stockrooms. But they are stockrooms to me because we keep the stock in them.

I have not learned the names of the parts yet. Neither have the girls on the line. One girl came up to the counter today and said, "I want ten ships of those little do-jiggers up there," pointing to the box she meant. I showed them to her. "No," she said, "that's the right side, I want the left. It's in the next box." I pulled out the next bin. "That's it," she said, "now I have to have the little curly-cue and that straight piece that goes on them."

"You better come find them," I told her.... What she actually got was a lever, a spring, and two angles, for each assembly.

July 17, 1943. One of the problems, or perhaps I should say one of the adjustments we are going to have to face when this war is over, is the equality of races. Where we have lived, we have had no contact with the colored race. . . .

More and more colored people, both men and women, are coming into the plant. They are working side by side with the whites, and who is to say they are not doing their share in winning the war....

From: *Ladies in Pants: A Home Front Diary* by Mable R. Gerken (New York: Exposition Press, 1949).

Rationing, Sacrifice, and Escape

American society in the early 1940s was a reflection of a nation at war. The country was suddenly plunged into a conflict that deeply affected everyone's life on a daily basis. Men were drafted into the military and women took civilian jobs to earn money and keep America's businesses working. Taxes were increased to pay the huge costs of a 16-million-person armed force, and other resources were diverted to the military and away from consumer goods.

Rationing became a way of life. In place of unlimited freedom to buy gasoline, Americans were given ration coupons that allowed them a certain amount of gas each month. Some foods—meat and sugar, for example—were also rationed through the use of coupons.

A young boy presents his war ration coupons to get food (*National Archives*).

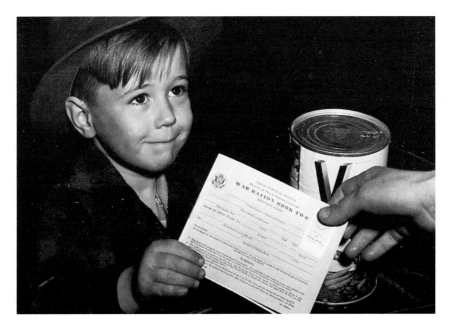

Comedian Bob Hope entertains American troops in 1944 (*Wide World Photos*).

The military's need for nylon for parachutes and other items led to a change in fashion. Without nylons, women began to wear pants or short socks. At times, they even went bare-legged.

Popular entertainment was also affected by the war. Many Hollywood directors were drafted into the military, where they used their skills to make propaganda films denouncing the evil "Huns" (Germans) and "Japs" and encouraging Americans to fight on to total victory. Popular entertainers—Frank Sinatra, Bob Hope, and the Andrews Sisters, for example— traveled to American bases in England and the Pacific to entertain GI's (members of the armed forces).

During such a period of sacrifice and stress, with the country threatened by a war whose duration was unknown, people sought escape in entertainment. The songs of the period were ballads filled with romance and longing, with a yearning for the day when the soldier would come home to his loving family.

Although the 1940s are now a half-century in the past, much of the culture of the time remains. Fashion innovations of the period—high shoulder pads or ankle socks, for example—reappear from time to time. The films of the World War II era are often seen in theaters. And Bob Hope—now in his 90s—was still entertaining the troops during the Persian Gulf War in 1991.

The early 1940s showed again that war is much more than a series of battles on a battlefield. It also affects every aspect of daily life on the home front.

In the selection that follows, Sheril Cunning remembers the early years of the war as a young girl in Long Beach, California. She recalls the excitement of the period and the strong feelings of patriotism that united all Americans.

Remembering an Era of Hope

We'd open up *Life* magazine and there were all those pictures of bombed-out Europe. One image after another of children in rags, huddled. I was just beginning to read. We thought any minute we could be like that, too. They could get us to eat our dinner, make us behave, do anything we didn't want to do—it was just: "Think of those kids in *Life* magazine, think how lucky you are."

My mother and all the neighbors would get together around the dining-room table, and they'd be changing a sugar coupon for a bread or a meat coupon. It was like a giant Monopoly game. It was quite exciting to have all the neighbors over and have this trading and bargaining. It was like the New York Stock Exchange. (Laughs) This was our social life.... There was a spirit of camaraderie.

Long Beach was a military town. There were several parades a year. We'd have miles and miles of tanks driving down Pine Avenue and everybody standing and cheering and clapping and waving flags. It was a constant reminder of this mighty strength and everything was going to be all right.

Some people were looking back at World War Two and saying that a lot of it was Hollywood and Madison Avenue. It took maybe twenty years to look back and say, Hey, what was all this? All these Hollywood musicals, keeping everybody's spirits up. I hear a Kate Smith record today and I just get all mush inside. That was the essence of America, Kate Smith singing "God Bless America." The patriotism was so thick you could cut it with a knife.

Immediately after the war was this rush: We're never gonna suffer again, we're gonna have everything bigger and better, and we're gonna build, build, build. Long Beach had been a very small town at the beginning of World War Two. You could get in a car and drive only three miles and you were out in the orange groves. Long Beach grew enormously after the war. And they built those teensy little tract houses all over everything and they didn't fall down.

From: *"The Good War": An Oral History of World War II* by Studs Terkel. Copyright © 1984 by Studs Terkel. Reprinted by permission of Pantheon Books, a division of Random House, Inc.

CHAPTER 4

THE PROMISE
OF PEACE

Harry S Truman, portrait by American painter Greta Kempton (*National Portrait Gallery*).

The Truman Way

Harry S Truman (1884-1972) became the 33rd President of the United States on the afternoon of April 12, 1945. Earlier that day, Franklin D. Roosevelt, who had been president since 1933, died of a stroke at his retreat in Warm Springs, Georgia.

Until 1944, when the Democrats selected him to be Roosevelt's vice-presidential running mate, Truman had been a two-term U.S. senator from Missouri. Truman knew Roosevelt was in ill health and would probably not survive his full fourth presidential term. In his memoirs, Truman describes being summoned to the White House late on the afternoon of the 12th to see Mrs. Roosevelt, who then says with great sympathy, "Harry, the president is dead."

Truman always had the capacity to make a decision quickly and then not worry needlessly over it. That same quality of self-assurance helped Truman through all of the momentous decisions he had to make during his 7 1/2 years as president. Perhaps the most agonizing was the decision to drop atomic bombs on the Japanese cities of Hiroshima and Nagasaki in August 1945—a decision that brought a quick end to the war. Later in life, Truman would rarely discuss the atomic bomb decision, but he insisted that once he had decided to use these powerful weapons, he never looked back.

Truman was president from 1945 until 1953, a critical period when the nation was making a difficult transition from war to peacetime. He faced enormous economic problems at home and the beginnings of what came to be called the "Cold War" (increasing political tensions) with the Soviet Union. Although he was frequently unpopular during his presidency—probably because of his stubborn and brusque manner—he is today considered one of America's great presidents.

Truman Remembers Roosevelt's Death

Sam [Rayburn, Speaker of the House of Representatives] told me that Steve Early [Roosevelt's press secretary] had called and wanted me to call right back. I did, and Early said to come right over to the White House and to come to the front entrance, and he said to come up to Mrs. Roosevelt's suite on the second floor. I didn't think much about it. I just supposed that the President had come back

from Georgia and was going to be at Bishop
Atwood's funeral. [Julius W. Atwood, the former
Episcopal Bishop of Arizona, was a friend of
Roosevelt's.] Roosevelt was an honorary pallbearer,
and I just supposed that was what had happened.

"And so I went over to the White House, and
Mrs. Roosevelt . . . Mrs. Roosevelt . . . she told me
that . . . the President . . . was dead."

From: Merle Miller, *Plain Speaking: An Oral Biography of Harry S
Truman* (New York: Berkley, 1974). Reprinted by permission.

The Soldiers Come Home

World War II ended officially on September 2, 1945, when the Japanese signed the document of surrender aboard the *U.S.S. Missouri* in Tokyo Bay. Over the next few months, millions of American men were discharged from military service to return to civilian life.

Some had been in the service for more than three years and most had not seen their families or homes during that time. Military life had been organized and guided by rules and regulations. A soldier had no control over his destiny, and his life was often in danger. Many had never left their hometowns before, but during the war had been in strange and dangerous places with names like Saipan and Iwo Jima or in historic cities of Europe.

An American soldier greets his daughter upon returning home from war (*Wide World Photos*).

After years of dangerous and dramatic living, what would it feel like to return home? The U.S. government faced the large problem of employment for these ex-servicemen. With the war's end, most of the women who had gone into the workforce returned to their roles as homemakers in order to allow the men to return to their jobs. (It was not until the 1970s that women began to return to the workplace in large numbers.)

Anticipating that many returning servicemen would need some kind of help, Congress passed a series of measures that together were known as the "GI Bill." These laws provided different kinds of assistance for ex-GI's, including low-interest loans for those who wanted to go back to college or secure mortgages to build homes.

Given the enormous numbers of soldiers involved, the transition from military to civilian life generally went smoothly over the years. In the selection printed here, James Fahey, a young sailor who served for three years on the *Montpelier,* describes his discharge from the navy in December 1945 and recounts his feelings during his first days at home after an absence of almost four years.

A Return to Normal Life

We arrived at San Diego, December 1, 1945. The United States was a sight for sore eyes.

They had a band and five girls at the bandstand to greet the ship as it pulled alongside the pier. Some of the crews' families were there to greet them. There was a large sign that said, "Welcome Home Veterans," "Well Done." The men who live in this part of the country will leave the ship here.

We remained at San Diego for three days and then left for New York. We passed through the Panama Canal on our way to New York.... After traveling for twelve days we reached Sandy Hook, New York.* We stayed there two days unloading all of our ammunition. Tuesday morning at 7 A.M., December 18, 1945, we docked at the Brooklyn Navy Yard. It took us 33 days to travel from Japan to New York. Our journey covered 14,000 miles.

I left New York for Boston where I was discharged from the Navy. A few days before Christmas I was a civilian once again. It was a very cold winter's night when I was discharged from the Naval Separation Center in Boston. When I walked in on my sister and her mother-in-law, Mrs. Sweeney, you could have knocked them over with a feather. They did not know I was in the States. Both of them put their arms around me and gave me a big kiss.

It felt great to be a civilian again but it did not seem like the war was over. For some time after, I would catch myself trying to conserve water. I would not let the water run, only when using it. After having water hours in the Pacific, it took some time before I got away from it. There were other habits I caught myself doing. It was quite a treat to sleep in a bed for a change with a roof over my head instead of a steel deck with your clothes on and never knowing when the rain would send you running for cover.

This will be my first Christmas in the States in four years and the best Christmas gift I ever received.

*Editor's Note: Sandy Hook is actually located in northeastern New Jersey, near Lower New York Bay.

From: James J. Fahey, *Pacific War Diary, 1942-1945* (Boston: Houghton Mifflin, 1992, originally published in 1963). Reprinted by permission.

Churchill Defines an Age

In early 1946, Winston Churchill, wartime prime minister of Great Britain, was unemployed. To his great surprise, he had been voted out of office in an election the year earlier at the very moment he was meeting with President Truman and Soviet leader Stalin in Potsdam, Germany.

Churchill had spent the first year of his forced retirement writing history books and thinking about the worsening relations between the United States, Britain, and their former ally, the Soviet Union.

In March 1946, Churchill, at the invitation of President Truman, journeyed to the small town of Fulton, Missouri. There, at Westminster College, he delivered one of the most famous and influential speeches of the postwar era—an address that came to be known as the "Iron Curtain" speech.

The name came from a line in the address in which Churchill warned that "From Stettin in the Baltic to Trieste in the Adriatic, an iron curtain has descended across the continent." Churchill was referring to all those countries of Eastern Europe that had fallen under the influence of the Soviet Union and in which Communist governments friendly to Moscow were being installed.

Churchill warned his audience about the growing power and threat that such a huge Soviet empire posed to Western Europe and the United States. His speech was widely publicized and helped convince Americans that the Soviets were a real threat to national security.

Because of this speech, the phrase, "behind the Iron Curtain" came to stand for all Soviet-dominated Communist countries of Eastern Europe.

"An Iron Curtain Has Descended"

From Stettin in the Baltic to Trieste in the Adriatic, an iron curtain has descended across the Continent. Behind that line lie all the capitals of the ancient states of Central and Eastern Europe. Warsaw, Berlin, Prague, Vienna, Budapest, Belgrade, Bucharest and Sofia, all these famous cities and the populations around them lie in what I must call the Soviet sphere, and all are subject in one form or another, not only to Soviet influence but to a very high and, in many cases, increasing measure of control from Moscow. Athens alone—Greece with its immortal glories—is free to decide its future at an election under British, American, and French observation. The Russian-dominated Polish Government has been encouraged to make enormous and wrongful inroads upon Germany, and mass expulsions of millions of Germans on a scale grievous or undreamed-of are now taking place. The Communist parties, which were very small in all these Eastern States of Europe, have been raised to pre-eminence and power far beyond their numbers and are seeking everywhere to obtain totalitarian control. Police governments are prevailing in nearly every case, and so far, except in Czechoslovakia, there is no true democracy.

From: Winston Churchill's "Iron Curtain" Speech, Fulton, Missouri, March, 1946.

Fighting the Communist Threat

In 1946, Communist guerrillas in Greece launched an all-out civil war against their elected government. British troops had been stationed in Greece since the end of the war in 1945, but the British informed the United States that they did not have the resources needed to help defeat the Greek Communists.

President Truman was greatly alarmed by the Greek civil war. He feared that if the Communists triumphed in Greece, neighboring Turkey and the countries of the Middle East would be threatened by Soviet influence. In addition, a victory in Greece would strengthen Communist parties in Italy and France and threaten democracy in Western Europe.

Truman decided to make a direct personal appeal to the Congress for financial assistance to Greece and Turkey. Taking the advice of a friendly Republican senator, Truman decided to "scare the heck out of them." His address to Congress, on March 12, 1947, painted a frightening picture of what would happen if the Greek Communists were allowed to overthrow the democratic government. The Congress quickly authorized an aid package to Greece and Turkey of some $300 million.

The policy of nonmilitary support to countries trying to resist Communist takeover came to be known as the "Truman Doctrine." The action by Congress on Greece and Turkey also reversed a trend of decreasing foreign aid that had occurred in the two years immediately after the war. From 1947 on, the American government, regardless of who was president, tried to assist foreign governments in their resistance to Communism from within.

The Truman Doctrine

It is necessary only to glance at a map to realize that the survival and integrity of the Greek nation are of grave importance in a much wider situation. If Greece should fall under the control of an armed minority, the effect upon its neighbor, Turkey, would be immediate and serious. Confusion and disorder might well spread throughout the entire Middle East.

Moreover, the disappearance of Greece as an independent state would have a profound effect upon those countries in Europe whose peoples are struggling against great difficulties to maintain their freedoms and their independence while they repair the damages of war.

It would be an unspeakable tragedy if these countries, which have struggled so long against overwhelming odds, should lose that victory for which they sacrificed so much. Collapse of free institutions and loss of independence would be disastrous not only for them but for the world. Discouragement and possibly failure would quickly be the lot of neighboring peoples striving to maintain their freedom and independence.

Should we fail to aid Greece and Turkey in this fateful hour, the effect will be far-reaching to the West as well as to the East.

We must take immediate and resolute action.

From: Harry S Truman's Speech to Congress, March 12, 1947. Transcription by U.S. Government Printing Office.

An Election Surprise

Most professional politicians, both Democrats and Republicans, believed that Harry S Truman could not win re-election in 1948. The Democrats had been in power since 1933, and most people seemed ready for a change.

The Republicans nominated the youthful Governor Thomas E. Dewey (1902-1971) of New York, who had run a respectable race against Franklin Roosevelt in the 1944 presidential election. Dewey and his advisors believed that all he had to do to win the presidency was to coast along and not say anything controversial. Public opinion polls taken during the summer of 1948 seemed to confirm this approach.

The re-elected Harry Truman celebrates his "surprise" victory by holding up a newspaper that published its election results too soon (*National Archives*).

Truman refused to believe that he would lose. To prove his vigorous commitment to a fighting campaign, he embarked on a number of "whistle-stop" train trips across the country. Typically, Truman's train would stop in a small town and the president would appear on the open platform of the last car to briefly address the crowd that gathered to welcome him. Sometimes his wife Bess and daughter Margaret would also appear.

The whistle-stop campaign, which is described by an observer in the selection printed here, was a significant factor in Truman's dramatic victory in 1948.

Remembering the Whistle Stops

It was to be a 21,928-mile trip, the most exhaustive campaign on land in history. An estimated 12 to 15 million Americans came out to see him and listened to 275 prepared speeches and as Truman put it, "about 200 more off the record." . . .

In Dexter, Iowa, Truman made his major speech of the tour before 75,000 persons at the national plowing contest. After a stodgy formal talk, he returned to the platform to speak off-the-cuff as a fellow farmer. "I can plow a straight furrow," he said. He described how he used to seed a 160-acre wheat field "without leaving a skip." He went on to brag that he did all this with only four mules and a gangplow, not the tractors of the modern era. The farmers whooped and hollered. . . .

After a while, the routine became standardized. At each stop the local high school band blared out "Hail to the Chief"; then came the presentation of a gift to Truman, his modest thank you, a welcome to local Democratic leaders and compliments to the community for its new factory or airfield. The climax was an attack on Republicans and the 80th Congress. . . .

After his political talk, he asked the crowd, "Howja like to meet my family?" Bess came on the back platform and he identified her as "the boss," with a broad wink at the men in the audience. Then he brought out Margaret and introduced her as "my baby" and "the boss's boss." This was the biggest hit at each stop. .. .

While Truman continued to make his way east, Dewey was proceeding according to his plan. With the polls showing him a certain victor, Dewey saw no need to extend himself. He rose late each day and limited his speaking. Truman was up at dawn and drove himself relentlessly until midnight, one day making a total of 16 speeches. Dewey radiated confidence, while Truman personified the underdog who needed everyone's help. Dewey cooed: Truman berated. Dewey exuded calm; Truman, an intense excitement. Dewey's campaign operated with clock-work efficiency; Truman's had an off-the-cuff informality.

From: Alfred Steinberg, *The Man from Missouri: The Life and Times of Harry S Truman* (New York: Putnam's, 1962).

Truman's speeches from the train were usually blunt attacks against his opponent and the "do-nothing" Republican-controlled Congress. While Dewey tried to appear as a dignified statesman, Truman went on the attack. Still, few people believed he would win.

Much to everyone's surprise—except Truman's—he did win. On the morning after the election, from the same platform where he had campaigned, Truman had the pleasure of holding up the front page of the *Chicago Tribune* that had printed the "results" of the election too early. It read, "Dewey Defeats Truman." Truman's broad smile revealed the great joy he felt at proving that he'd been right all along.

FROM WORLD WAR II TO THE RE-ELECTION OF TRUMAN: 1939–1948

1939
Adolf Hitler invades Poland. World War II begins in Europe.

1940
Japan allies with Nazi Germany and makes plans to dominate East Asia. The U.S. government imposes an oil embargo on Japan.

1941
The Japanese bomb U.S. warships at Pearl Harbor. President Roosevelt asks Congress to declare war on Japan.

1942
President Roosevelt orders the evacuation of Japanese Americans from the West Coast to concentration camps.

1942–1943
Colonel James Doolittle leads the first American bombing raid on Tokyo. Allied troops initiate Operation Torch in North Africa.

1944
Led by Supreme Commander Dwight D. Eisenhower, the Western Allied Forces land on the beaches of Normandy; D-Day had come for German occupied France.

1945
The United States drops atomic bombs on the Japanese cities of Hiroshima and Nagasaki. Japan surrenders and the war ends.

1946–1947
Winston Churchill gives his "Iron Curtain Speech" and warns of growing Soviet power. President Truman says that America should aid countries in fighting communism; his idea becomes the Truman Doctrine.

1948
President Truman embarks on "whistle–stop" campaigning trips and wins re–election.

FOR FURTHER READING

Adler, David. *We Remember the Holocaust*. New York: Henry Holt & Co., 1989.

Bliven, Bruce, Jr. *The Story of D-Day*. New York: Random House Books for Young Readers, 1981.

Cannon, Marian G. *Dwight David Eisenhower: War Hero & President*. New York: Watts, 1990.

Collins, David R. *Harry S Truman: People's President*. New York: Chelsea House, 1991.

Cross, Robin. *Roosevelt: And the Americans at War*. New York: Watts, 1990.

Darby, Jean. *Douglas MacArthur*. Minneapolis: Lerner, 1989.

Devaney, John. *America Turns the Tide, 1943*. New York: Walker & Co., 1992.

_____. *Franklin Delano Roosevelt, President*. New York: Walker & Co., 1987

Driemen, J. E. *An Unbreakable Spirit: A Biography of Winston Churchill*. New York: Macmillian Children's Book Group, 1990.

Morimoto, Junko. *My Hiroshima*. New York: Puffin Books, 1992.

Nardo, Don. *World War Two: The War in the Pacific*. San Diego: Lucent Books, 1991.

O'Neal, Michael. *President Truman & the Atomic Bomb: Opposing Viewpoints*. San Diego: Greenhaven, 1990.

Skipper, G. C. *Pearl Harbor*. Chicago: Childrens Press, 1983.

Stein, R. Conrad. *Home Front*. Chicago: Childrens Press, 1986.

Index